A
HEARTBEAT
FROM
ETERNITY

Dr. Carlton L. Burford

ISBN 978-1-969865-38-1 (Paperback)
ISBN 978-1-969865-39-8 (Ebook)

Inquiries and Book Orders should be addressed to:

Leavitt Peak Press
17901 Pioneer Blvd Ste L #298,
Artesia, California 90701
Phone #: 2092191548

Table of Contents

Chapter 1

Overview

Wow. There are over 8.2 billion people living in the world currently. 8.2 billion people on various continents, living in a number of countries, separated by oceans, lakes, and rivers. 8.2 billion people that are diverse in language, skin color, social systems, and religions. People that are diverse in cultural norms and age groups. People that are different in educational achievement and occupational positions.

In spite of all of these differences, there is one thing we all have in common – we are all just a heartbeat from eternity.

As I am writing this booklet, approximately 150,000 people worldwide cross the threshold from life to death every day, each was probably not aware they were a heartbeat from eternity. I pray they were all saved so they can spend eternity with God. Thank God there are over 350,000 births per day, worldwide, to keep the population growing.

I know some people would love to live in this world forever, taking in all it offers. They love going to fancy restaurants, staying in luxurious hotels and resorts. They love getting a tan on a beautiful beach or visiting some of the great sites in the world. All I can say is enjoy it while you can but keep the thought in the back of your mind that you are just a heartbeat from eternity.

There are individuals attending church services and activities, participating in fraternity and sorority functions, enjoying family reunions and picnics, engaging in outreach, evangelistic and Biblical-based studies which can all be positive and great. However, those activities do not exempt you from being a heartbeat from eternity.

Each week, for the past 13 years, I have been publishing a newsletter on worldwide earth changes, including volcanic activities, earthquakes, weather and solar activities, animal deaths and animal attacks, as well as other areas. Each week I see articles of people killed in earthquakes, storms, hurricanes and tornadoes. I see articles of people mauled to death by dogs, bears, lions and other wildlife. I see people killed by tsunamis and smoldering heat or super cold temperatures. On top of that, daily we see news stories about senseless killings and war victims.

I wonder how many knew when they woke up in the morning it would be their last day on earth. How many had even thought about the fact that they were just a heartbeat from eternity.

But what is eternity? Simply put, it is timelessness. What we know as time is merely a subset of eternity. God, alone, exists in eternity (*Isaiah 57:15 says "For thus says the High and Lofty One Who inhabits eternity, whose name is Holy: "I dwell in the high and holy place ..." NKJV*). God had no beginning and has no end. On the contrary, we all had a period where we didn't exist, but after conception we entered this phenomenon called time. However, at the end of our time on earth, we will enter into eternity. The reality is that we are all just a heartbeat from that eternity.

It doesn't matter if you are rich or poor, have an elementary school education or a PhD, we are all just a heartbeat from eternity.

The number of possessions you have or the amount of money and wealth you have accumulated will not change the fact that we are all just a heartbeat from eternity.

How many of us think about that as we leave home for work or are playing with our children or going shopping for our favorite treats. As adults we don't normally think about it, as teenagers, we think about it even less, and surely as children, we don't think about it at all, but it does not alter the reality that we are all just a heartbeat from eternity.

So, what is the purpose of me bringing to mind something we usually don't want to think about? Well, one day we will all cross that boundary from life, in time, to existence in eternity. Hebrews 9:27 says *"And as it is appointed unto men once to die, but after this the judgment:" (KJV)*.

My concern is that where you spend eternity is determined by what state you were in when you entered therein. That is, did you enter eternity as a "saved" person or an "unsaved" person. That is a decision which you, and only you, must make while you are living in this period called time. I want to make sure you think about this reality now and make the choice to be "saved" before leaving this world.

If you enter eternity as a "saved" person, you will spend eternity with God. If you are an unsaved person at the moment of transition, you will spend eternity separated from God eventually in a place called "outer darkness" also called "the Lake of Fire" or eternal hell, where there is weeping and gnashing of teeth.

So, what do I mean about a "saved" person or an "unsaved" person, the lake of fire and spending eternity with God. I will let the Bible answer those questions and realities, using the New King James Version of the Bible.

Chapter 2

What is a "saved" person?

As this question is asked, it is important to understand there are a host of religions in the world: Christianity, Islam, Judaism, Buddhism, Hinduism, Shinto, Confucianism, Taoism and so on. Each has their god and pathway to get to him. Some even say we are all worshipping the same god. That is as far from the truth as one can get. There is but one true and living God who exist in three Persons (The Father, The Son (Jesus), and the Holy Spirit) - Three Persons in the Godhead. Consider the following scriptures:

Jeremiah 10:10

> *10 But the Lord is the true God; He is the living God and the everlasting King. At His wrath the earth will tremble, And the nations will not be able to endure His indignation.*
>
> *NKJV*

John 6:67-69

> *67 Then Jesus said to the twelve, "Do you also want to go away?"*

68 But Simon Peter answered Him, "Lord, to whom shall we go? You have the words of eternal life.

69 Also we have come to believe and know that You are the Christ, the Son of the living God."

NKJV

John 20:26-31

26 And after eight days His disciples were again inside, and Thomas with them. Jesus came, the doors being shut, and stood in the midst, and said, "Peace to you!"

27 Then He said to Thomas, "Reach your finger here, and look at My hands; and reach your hand here, and put it into My side. Do not be unbelieving, but believing."

28 And Thomas answered and said to Him, "My Lord and my God!"

29 Jesus said to him, "Thomas, because you have seen Me, you have believed. Blessed are those who have not seen and yet have believed."

30 And truly Jesus did many other signs in the presence of His disciples, which are not written in this book;

31 but these are written that you may believe that Jesus is the Christ, the Son of God, and that believing you may have life in His name.

NKJV

Christianity is the only religion that our God, who is a Spirit that created all things, and is all-powerful, all-knowing, eternal, and is everywhere present at the same time, also became part of His own creation by also being born into the world He created in the person of the Man, Jesus of Nazareth. Never did He cease to be God, who is a Spirit, but He also put on human flesh. He did this because the man He originally created as innocent and without sin (Adam) disobeyed God and thus became a sinner by nature (original sin).

God created man for His own good pleasure to enjoy fellowship with him. Revelation 4:11 says *"Thou art worthy, O Lord, to receive glory and honour and power: for thou hast created all things, and for thy pleasure they are and were created"* (KJV). God is a holy God and separates Himself from sin, thus, to regain full fellowship with man, He required innocent human blood to atone for the sins of the entire human race. Since a Man sinned in the beginning, God required a sinless Man, not an animal, to redeem Man back to God.

Though there were good men who were born, they were all born sinners by birth, since their fathers were sinners. Men like Enoch, Noah, Seth, Abraham, Isaac, Jacob, Joseph, Moses, Joshua, Samuel, David, Solomon, Isaiah, Jeremiah, Daniel, Ezekiel all had their positive moments in history but were still born with the original sin of Adam.

So, there was a dilemma. How can a sinless man die to redeem us all back to God when all people born into this world are born with the original sin of Adam and are thus born sinners?

The solution God had already planned before creating the world was that He, Himself, though the Holy Spirit, would also become flesh by being born into this world through a virgin young woman (Mary). Consider the following scriptures:

John 1:1-4

> *1 In the beginning was the Word, and the Word was with God, and the Word was God.*

2 He was in the beginning with God.

3 All things were made through Him, and without Him nothing was made that was made.

4 In Him was life, and the life was the light of men.

NKJV

John 1:14

14 And the Word became flesh and dwelt among us, and we beheld His glory, the glory as of the only begotten of the Father, full of grace and truth.

NKJV

2 Corinthians 5:18-19

18 Now all things are of God, who has reconciled us to Himself through Jesus Christ, and has given us the ministry of reconciliation,

19 that is, that God was in Christ reconciling the world to Himself, not imputing their trespasses to them, and has committed to us the word of reconciliation.

NKJV

So, it was Jesus of Nazareth, God's only begotten Son, who was born into the world He created as a sinless human being. In fact, the true purpose of Him being born into this world was to die for the sins of the world. Speaking of His crucifixion Jesus said the following in John 12:27: *"Now is my soul troubled; and what shall I say?*

Father, save me from this hour: but for this cause came I unto this hour." (KJV)

Jesus substituted Himself for sinful man by the shedding of His innocent blood on the cross that He may reconcile all who believe in Him back to God. The key here is that a person must believe who Jesus is (the Son of the Living God), that He died for your sins but was raised from the dead as the Son of God with power and repent of your sins.

Consider the following scriptures:

Romans 3:23

> *23 for all have sinned and fall short of the glory of God,*

> *NKJV*

Romans 5:6-9

> *6 For when we were still without strength, in due time Christ died for the ungodly.*

> *7 For scarcely for a righteous man will one die; yet perhaps for a good man someone would even dare to die.*

> *8 But God demonstrates His own love toward us, in that while we were still sinners, Christ died for us.*

> *9 Much more then, having now been justified by His blood, we shall be saved from wrath through Him.*

> *NKJV*

Romans 5:19

> *19 For as by one man's disobedience many were made sinners, so also by one Man's obedience many will be made righteous.*

> *NKJV*

Hebrews 9:11-14

> *11 But Christ came as High Priest of the good things to come, with the greater and more perfect tabernacle not made with hands, that is, not of this creation.*

> *12 Not with the blood of goats and calves, but with His own blood He entered the Most Holy Place once for all, having obtained eternal redemption.*

> *13 For if the blood of bulls and goats and the ashes of a heifer, sprinkling the unclean, sanctifies for the purifying of the flesh,*

> *14 how much more shall the blood of Christ, who through the eternal Spirit offered Himself without spot to God, cleanse your conscience from dead works to serve the living God?*

> *NKJV*

In conclusion, Jesus was born into this world to save us all from the penalty of sin – eternal death. However, only those who believe in Him (who He is, His death, His burial, His resurrection) will be covered by His blood and be declared righteous by God Himself.

Romans 5:8-9

8 But God demonstrates His own love toward us, in that while we were still sinners, Christ died for us. 9 Much more then, having now been justified by His blood, we shall be saved from wrath through Him.

NKJV

John 3:16-18

16 For God so loved the world that He gave His only begotten Son, that whoever believes in Him should not perish but have everlasting life.

17 For God did not send His Son into the world to condemn the world, but that the world through Him might be saved.

18 "He who believes in Him is not condemned; but he who does not believe is condemned already, because he has not believed in the name of the only begotten Son of God.

NKJV

I know that was a lot of scriptures, but I want to make sure you see just how important Jesus' substitutionary atoning death meant to God. It is those individuals who have placed their faith and trust in Jesus Christ as their Lord and personal Savior who are "saved."

Romans 10:9-13

9 that if you confess with your mouth the Lord Jesus and believe in your heart that God has raised Him from the dead, you will be saved.

10 For with the heart one believes unto righteousness, and with the mouth confession is made unto salvation.

11 For the Scripture says, "Whoever believes on Him will not be put to shame."

12 For there is no distinction between Jew and Greek, for the same Lord over all is rich to all who call upon Him.

13 For "whoever calls on the name of the Lord shall be saved."

NKJV

If you are not saved, just do the following in sincerity and in truth after hearing the Gospel.:

Plan of Salvation
(How To Be Saved)

1. **You must admit that you are a sinner, both by birth and by behavior**

    Romans 3:23

    23 for all have sinned and fall short of the glory of God,

    NKJV

    Romans 3:10

    10 As it is written: "There is none righteous, no, not one; "

DR. CARLTON L. BURFORD

NKJV

2. **You must recognize that sin carries a wage – Death (spiritual separation from God)**

Romans 6:23

> *23 For the wages of sin is death, but the gift of God is eternal life in Christ Jesus our Lord.*

NKJV

Romans 5:12

> *12 Therefore, just as through one man sin entered the world, and death through sin, and thus death spread to all men, because all sinned*

NKJV

This is when you repent of your sins.

3. **However, you can rejoice because God has provided a Substitute to die in your stead – Jesus.**

Romans 5:8

> *8 But God demonstrates His own love toward us, in that while we were still sinners, Christ died for us.*

NKJV

John 3:16-18

16 For God so loved the world that He gave His only begotten Son, that whoever believes in Him should not perish but have everlasting life.

17 For God did not send His Son into the world to condemn the world, but that the world through Him might be saved.

18 "He who believes in Him is not condemned; but he who does not believe is condemned already, because he has not believed in the name of the only begotten Son of God.

NKJV

4.   **In spite of all that God has done, there is still something YOU must do in conjunction of repenting of your sins!!!**

Romans 10:9-13

*9 that if you **confess with your mouth the Lord Jesus** and **believe in your heart that God has raised Him from the dead,** you will be saved.*

10 For with the heart one believes unto righteousness, and with the mouth confession is made unto salvation.

11 For the Scripture says, "Whoever believes on Him will not be put to shame."

12 For there is no distinction between Jew and Greek, for the same Lord over all is rich to all who call upon Him.

13 For "whoever calls on the name of the Lord shall be saved."

NKJV

After being saved, you need to be baptized and unite with a Bible-centered Church for teaching and fellowship with other believers.

However, even as a "saved" person, you are still one heartbeat from eternity but now you know where you will spend eternity – with God. Praise His Holy Name.

Chapter 3

What is an "unsaved" person?

Well, the simplest answer is that it is a person who is not "saved". If you have not accepted Jesus Christ as your Lord and Personal Savior, you are unsaved. Jesus makes it quite clear that the only way to get to the Father (God), and thus be saved, is thru Him.

John 14:6

> *6 Jesus said to him, "I am the way, the truth, and the life. No one comes to the Father except through Me.*
>
> *NKJV*

I know you may have heard other say there are many ways to get to heaven and many ways to God. Unfortunately, that is contrary to Biblical truth. Since Jesus is God in the flesh, surely, He would have known if there were other ways to get to God, or be saved. Yet, Jesus emphasized that He, and He alone, is the only way to the Father.

You know some people have the belief that God is some Old Person sitting on a throne just waiting for us to mess up by sinning just to send us to hell. The Bible presents God as just the opposite.

2 Peter 3:8-9

> *8 But, beloved, do not forget this one thing, that with the Lord one day is as a thousand years, and a thousand years as one day.*
>
> *9 The Lord is not slack concerning His promise, as some count slackness, but is longsuffering toward us, not willing that any should perish but that all should come to repentance.*
>
> *NKJV*

God, our heavenly Father, is a loving God who, when we could not save ourselves, sent His only begotten Son to die in our place as our substitute so that we can spend eternity with Him.

2 Corinthians 5:17-21

> *17 Therefore, if anyone is in Christ, he is a new creation; old things have passed away; behold, all things have become new.*
>
> *18 Now all things are of God, who has reconciled us to Himself through Jesus Christ, and has given us the ministry of reconciliation,*
>
> *19 that is, that God was in Christ reconciling the world to Himself, not imputing their trespasses to them, and has committed to us the word of reconciliation.*
>
> *20 Now then, we are ambassadors for Christ, as though God were pleading through us: we implore you on Christ's behalf, be reconciled to God.*

*21 For He made Him who knew no sin to be sin for
us, that we might become the righteousness of God
in Him.*

NKJV

However, God created us with free wills. He does not force us to do anything, including accepting His gift of salvation. This is a choice that you must make for yourself. Others can pray for you to make the decision for Jesus, but it is up to you, and you alone, to make the decision. Will you do it today?

Romans 6:23

*23 For the wages of sin is death, but the gift of God
is eternal life in Christ Jesus our Lord.*

NKJV

If you accept God's gift of salvation (Jesus Christ) as earlier explained, you will be "saved" and spend eternity with Him. If you fail to do so while living in this period we call time, while in our current bodies, you will be "unsaved". The choice is yours but please remember that time is running out. None of us know when we will experience our last heartbeat. But be informed that the way you enter eternity will be the way you will exist forever in eternity. With God (saved) or separated from God (unsaved). It's your choice.

Chapter 4

What is the "Lake of Fire"

Before I deal with this term, let me remind you that those who are "saved", will immediately be in the presence of God who is in heaven when they leave this life.

2 Corinthians 5:6-8

> *6 So we are always confident, knowing that while we are at home in the body we are absent from the Lord.*
>
> *7 For we walk by faith, not by sight.*
>
> *8 We are confident, yes, well pleased rather to be absent from the body and to be present with the Lord.*
>
> *NKJV*

On the other hand, those who are "unsaved" will immediately find themselves in *hades* (hell), the temporary holding place under the earth where they will be in torment and agony until right before the end of time when they will appear before Jesus at the Great White Throne judgment.

The temporary location of the "unsaved"

Luke 16:19-25

19 "There was a certain rich man who was clothed in purple and fine linen and fared sumptuously every day.

20 But there was a certain beggar named Lazarus, full of sores, who was laid at his gate,

21 desiring to be fed with the crumbs which fell from the rich man's table. Moreover the dogs came and licked his sores.

22 So it was that the beggar died, and was carried by the angels to Abraham's bosom. The rich man also died and was buried.

*23 And being in torments in **Hades**, he lifted up his eyes and saw Abraham afar off, and Lazarus in his bosom.*

24 "Then he cried and said, 'Father Abraham, have mercy on me, and send Lazarus that he may dip the tip of his finger in water and cool my tongue; for I am tormented in this flame.'

25 But Abraham said, 'Son, remember that in your lifetime you received your good things, and likewise Lazarus evil things; but now he is comforted and you are tormented.

NKJV

After death (their last heartbeat), the beggar entered eternity in Abraham's bosom, also called Paradise, which is now in heaven with God. However, the rich man entered eternity in hell, also known as *Shoel* or *hades*. This is his temporary dwelling place until he enters his final and permanent dwelling place, the Lake of Fire. See the following scriptures:

The permanent location of the "unsaved"

Revelation 20:11-15

> *11 Then I saw a great white throne and Him who sat on it, from whose face the earth and the heaven fled away. And there was found no place for them.*
>
> *12 And I saw the dead, small and great, standing before God, and books were opened. And another book was opened, which is the Book of Life. And the dead were judged according to their works, by the things which were written in the books.*
>
> *13 The sea gave up the dead who were in it, and Death and Hades delivered up the dead who were in them. And they were judged, each one according to his works.*
>
> *14 Then Death and Hades were cast into the lake of fire. This is the second death.*
>
> *15 And anyone not found written in the Book of Life was cast into the lake of fire.*
>
> *NKJV*

The Lake of Fire (sometimes known as *Gehenna*) is the permanent residence of all the "unsaved" over time. It will not reside underneath the present earth. It will be located in "Outer darkness" away from the earth and separated from God.

Matthew 25:30

> *30 And cast the unprofitable servant into the outer darkness. There will be weeping and gnashing of teeth.'*

> *NKJV*

Revelation 21:7-8

> *7 He who overcomes shall inherit all things, and I will be his God and he shall be My son.*

> *8 But the cowardly, unbelieving, abominable, murderers, sexually immoral, sorcerers, idolaters, and all liars shall have their part in the lake which burns with fire and brimstone, which is the second death."*

> *NKJV*

Whether you simply do not believe in God or are unsure whether there is a God or not, you are, per the Bible, unsaved and will spend eternity in the permanent location of the Lake of Fire.

No matter what your religious affiliation may be, if you have not accepted Jesus Christ as your Lord and Personal Savior, per the scripture, you are also unsaved and will spend eternity in the permanent location of the Lake of Fire.

You see Jesus is not just a good man or just a prophet. Neither is He the brother of Lucifer or a good teacher. He is not part Man and part God, or the archangel Michael reincarnated. Jesus **IS** God, along with The Father and The Holy Ghost. A concept we, as humans, cannot conceive with our limited minds, but a reality in the Godhead.

I beg and plead with you to reconsider your belief in Jesus Christ as your Lord and Savior before it is too late. Before your heart beats for the last time. For we are all just a heartbeat from eternity.

I would love to meet you in heaven as we spend eternity in the presence of the Living and True God. No more pain, no more suffering, no more hunger or thirst. No more murder or death. No more crying or sorrow.

I know this is hard to conceive based on the world we are currently living in, but Paul had this to say about our future abode with God"

1 Corinthians 2:9

9 But as it is written: "Eye has not seen, nor ear heard, Nor have entered into the heart of man The things which God has prepared for those who love Him."

NKJV

With all that said, please remember we are all just a heartbeat from eternity.

Chapter 5

What does it mean to spend eternity with God?

It means we will be in new bodies (glorified bodies) that are designed to live forever. We will have bodies like Jesus had after His resurrection. He could appear and disappear at will. He didn't have to, but He could eat and drink.

We will have bodies that will never grow old or get sick. We will be able to see God and fellowship with Him.

This current heaven and earth have been sin-stained, so God is going to destroy them and create a new heaven and a new earth with absolutely no sin it them.

We will be free of Satan, the fallen angels, evil spirits and demons. They will all be in the Lake of Fire.

We will have fellowship with our families, friends, people we may currently consider to be our enemies, and all who are saved (starting with Adam and Eve) for all eternity. Our minds will be renewed but not wiped clean. We will remember our loved ones and experiences while in our natural bodies. But above all, we will spend eternity with the True and Living God.

We will be in a complete state of bliss for ever and ever. Amen.

1 John 3:2

2 Beloved, now we are children of God; and it has not yet been revealed what we shall be, but we know that when He is revealed, we shall be like Him, for we shall see Him as He is.

NKJV

Revelation 21:1-5

21 Now I saw a new heaven and a new earth, for the first heaven and the first earth had passed away. Also there was no more sea.

2 Then I, John, saw the holy city, New Jerusalem, coming down out of heaven from God, prepared as a bride adorned for her husband.

3 And I heard a loud voice from heaven saying, "Behold, the tabernacle of God is with men, and He will dwell with them, and they shall be His people. God Himself will be with them and be their God.

4 And God will wipe away every tear from their eyes; there shall be no more death, nor sorrow, nor crying. There shall be no more pain, for the former things have passed away."

5 Then He who sat on the throne said, "Behold, I make all things new." And He said to me, "Write, for these words are true and faithful."

NKJV

Please don't put this booklet down or in your book collection without making sure you are saved. This is not the time to hesitate or put off the correct decision concerning Jesus.

Now is the time to make the correct decision so you can spend eternity with Him.

Hebrews 3:7-8

> *7 Therefore, as the Holy Spirit says: "Today, if you will hear His voice,*
>
> *8 Do not harden your hearts as in the rebellion, In the day of trial in the wilderness,*
>
> *NKJV*

Please keep in mind and tell others - we are all just a heartbeat from eternity.

2 Corinthians 13:14

> *14 The grace of the Lord Jesus Christ, and the love of God, and the communion of the Holy Spirit be with you all. Amen.*
>
> *NKJV*

www.ingramcontent.com/pod-product-compliance
Lightning Source LLC
Chambersburg PA
CBHW051253120626
46547CB00014B/1924